Beauty Beyond the Walls

SONORA BROWN

WESTBOW
PRESS°
A DIVISION OF THOMAS NELSON
& ZONDERVAN

WestBow Press books may be ordered through booksellers or by contacting:

WestBow Press
A Division of Thomas Nelson & Zondervan
1663 Liberty Drive
Bloomington, IN 47403
www.westbowpress.com
1 (866) 928-1240

Because of the dynamic nature of the Internet, any web addresses or links contained in this book may have changed since publication and may no longer be valid. The views expressed in this work are solely those of the author and do not necessarily reflect the views of the publisher, and the publisher hereby disclaims any responsibility for them.

Any people depicted in stock imagery provided by Thinkstock are models, and such images are being used for illustrative purposes only. Certain stock imagery © Thinkstock.

ISBN: 978-1-5127-9775-6 (sc)
ISBN: 978-1-5127-9776-3 (e)

Library of Congress Control Number: 2017911719

Print information available on the last page.

WestBow Press rev. date: 08/18/2017

For ease, in this book, I use "God" to mean the Trinity: Father, Son and Spirit. I use "Him," to reference God, though God transcends gender. God is far bigger than the English language and I hope the simplicity of the terminology will not denigrate or distract from the fullness of "I am who I am" (Exodus 3:14).

This book is dedicated to my parents, who taught me by example to know God.

Introduction

You received Christ Jesus, the Master;
now live *him. You're deeply rooted in him.*
You're well-constructed upon him. You know
your way around the faith. Now do what
you've been taught.
School's out; quit studying the subject and
start living *it!*
—Colossians 2:6–7, The Message

Sunshine peeked through the cracks of my bedroom blinds, announcing a new day. I slipped out of bed, and crept to the basement. I needed time alone with God. The past year had gone so well I started to feel disconnected from God. I missed the kind of closeness with Him I experienced in seasons of life when my need for Him was more pressing.

In six months, I would move to Afghanistan to intern at an NGO for my final semester of graduate school. I was also invited to help start a for-profit entity to import agricultural technology. Running a business was my dream, and if everything went well, I would stay indefinitely. Though I had prepared for this opportunity for more than six years, I didn't feel spiritually ready.

So I sought the One who brought me to this moment.

"Lord," I whispered, "I'm here, and I know you are too, but I don't feel anything. All the motions of life are bringing me closer to when I will put into action what You put in my heart. But I need more of You. I want to really know You."

My thoughts wandered ahead to a life I could not picture. I wondered if I had what it took, or if I'd fail.

In a holy moment, I heard God tell me, "It is accomplished."

Throughout my time in Afghanistan, I wondered what those words meant. By the end I knew. He was going to accomplish my request to know Him more.

This is my story.

1

My Peace I Leave with You

I arrived at the Philadelphia International Airport with two fifty-pound rolling suitcases, my laptop, and a handbag. It was all I could take to Afghanistan, yet weaving through cars, travelers, and curbs, the pride I felt about fitting everything into these small spaces no longer seemed like an accomplishment. I could barely carry them to the check-in desk.

I threw away my cell phone when I arrived at my gate. It clunked when it reached the bottom of the empty waste can, cementing the reality that I was disconnecting from everything familiar.

Sitting on the plane, I felt troubled. I opened my Bible to the Book of John and read, "Peace I leave with you; my peace I give to you. I do not give to you as the world gives. Do not let your hearts be troubled and do not let them be afraid" (14:27, NRSV).

I was afraid, not of kidnappings or bombings, but of

failure. I never felt like I failed at anything. Well, I failed my best friend once when she needed me. And I failed at every sport I attempted. But when I set out to succeed, I did. I passed classes with As. I planned trips and events to perfection. Failure wasn't an option.

In truth, I only got into situations in which I knew I could succeed. I liked feeling in control. Even though I know God is ultimately in control, I am most comfortable under the illusion that I am. But I knew when I stepped off the last plane into unfamiliar surroundings the safety of that guise would disappear, and require me to rely on God more than ever.

My Bible stayed open to Christ's gentle instruction from John, as I wrestled with my fears of failure and giving up control. By the time I landed, Jesus's consoling promise brought peace. It became my anchor for the years ahead.

2

My Movie Set

Arriving in Afghanistan was like stepping onto a movie set. The opening scene was a panoramic shot of a white, single-engine propeller plane. Desert winds blew up a bar of sand behind the aircraft, as it tossed and tottered until it thumped onto the runway.

"Welcome to Mazar-I-Sharif," announced the pilot in his Australian accent.

On the ground, I could just make out the outline of mountain peaks on the horizon through a dusty, sun-drenched haze. The simple mud buildings nearly convinced me the clock had rewound hundreds of years.

But I felt the grit of sand between my teeth and the power of the desert wind as I staggered across the tarmac. And then the heat; it jolted me back to reality. Life in Afghanistan would be nothing like a movie.

This became clearer when I arrived at the house I shared with three other international women. Compared to the average Afghan, we lived a Hollywood lifestyle. But as an American, I felt like a pioneer. Our only furniture was a table and chairs. We had electricity, but relied on a generator because the city power was usually out. Nothing was automatic or prepackaged—a stark contrast from my student life of cafeteria food, cereal, and microwave dinners. I didn't even know how to prepare a meal from scratch. We didn't have a microwave or coffee pot, so I learned to use a gas stove. In the winter, sawdust and wood stoves heated our main rooms. We reclined in our living room on traditional floor cushions, and entertained ourselves by watching DVDs on our television, or playing ping pong or guitar.

Figuring out life without appliances was just one of many changes and challenges. I still faced learning a new culture, language, job, and making friends. God had my rapt attention.

3

Dari 101

A well-intentioned American enrolled me in a beginner's Dari class my first week in Afghanistan. Dari is the more widely spoken of two official languages. Because only some of the educated males spoke English, I needed to know Dari to talk to the average Afghan. But starting classes so early in my arrival added to my new life stressors.

"As if I need another challenge right now," I muttered, dragging myself to class. The two other students, American women my age, were already a few lessons ahead of me. They seemed more eager and confident than I felt. "I'm behind before I've even started," I thought. This was unfamiliar territory.

The class sat in a circle of plastic chairs, sipping Nescafé and waiting for our teacher to arrive. I looked up from my drink to see an Afghan woman coming down the stairs. She wore a burqa; the front was lifted over her head, revealing her fully clothed body, and mass of blue fabric draped behind her.

Had I seen her wearing jeans and a T-shirt and heard her speaking English, I would not have known she was Afghan. But here she was, wearing her half-up burqa—a look so foreign to me.

"Salaam Alekum. Chi hal doren?" she greeted me.

I didn't understand what she said. I didn't know what to do. Look at her? Say hello in English? Extend my hand? I intended to befriend Afghan women, but at first sight, Aisha, my Dari teacher, intimidated me. And so did my first few months of lessons.

"Gayloss," she said as she pointed to a cup.

"Saib," she said as she pointed to an apple.

"Chowkey," she said as she pointed to a chair.

Aisha repeated the names of each object and we pointed to the correct one. By the end of each lesson, I thought I was catching on, but by the next morning's lesson, I forgot much of what I learned.

With time, the Dari words became more familiar, as did the sight of Aisha in her half-up burqa. Her calm and encouraging demeanor relaxed me. The pleasant lines on her young but weathered face revealed a kindness that a difficult life could not take from her. The tone and cadence of her voice reverberated in my thoughts long after our lessons ended.

Aisha's home was close to mine, so we visited each other in our free time. I got to know her mother, husband, and children. When my Dari improved, we moved to individual sessions at my house. The lessons evolved into conversations over coffee and chocolate. She wanted to know what it was like to drive a car, and I wanted to know what it was like to live in Taliban times. She described giving birth without medical care, and I described having my wisdom teeth removed under the influence of laughing gas. She explained how she was treated as a second wife, and I explained how I was treated as the supervisor of Afghan men. On my birthdays, Aisha made my favorite Afghan dessert, delivered by one of her six children. I celebrated her religious holidays with her family, and she celebrated mine. In the summer, her family invited me to picnics in the park. When I got sick, Aisha sat next to me with my head in her lap, and tenderly stroked my hair while she talked about her life.

We laughed a lot, but after each lesson, the gravity of our vastly difference circumstances weighed heavily on my heart. Aisha's life was nothing like mine, but our differences didn't form walls between us. Instead, they became the foundation for a beautiful friendship.

4

Call Me Koko

The day I arrived, an old man dressed in worn clothes opened the gate and greeted me with a big smile and words I didn't understand. He took my luggage and carried it to my second-story bedroom.

"Is he our guard?" I asked my housemate. I didn't see another man around, and it was common for foreigners to employ guards in their homes. But this wasn't the able-bodied, rifle-toting man in uniform I'd pictured.

"Oh yes," she confirmed. "A very trusted man. We have three of them who rotate twelve-hour shifts, 365 days a year. We call them all *koko*, which means uncle."

Although our guards did not carry guns, they officially protected us and our house, deterring break-ins while we were away, and serving as a warden for us young women separated from our male relatives. They regarded us as family, too, by caring for us as they would their nieces, which I discovered soon after my arrival when I caught a head cold.

That day, I stayed home from work. When koko didn't

see me leave at the appointed time, he politely knocked on our inside door. He respectfully lowered his head when I answered the door; he didn't know how I was dressed. While my baggy pants and T-shirt were acceptable to wear at home, I stood partially behind the door anyway.

"*Salaam*," I said, my voice hoarse. He started talking and making gestures. But he could see I didn't understand.

"*Choi*," (tea) he finally said, as he made a drinking motion and rubbed his hand on his throat. I nodded, thanked him, and closed the door.

"*Choi*. Of course," I thought, "their antidote for everything."

Drinking tea didn't do as much for my sore throat as his kindness.

As our kokos proved their good intentions, I increasingly relied on them, and they became an integral part of my cultural adjustment. I needed a warden, a fire starter, a dish washer when we hosted guests, and a delivery service after dark. They advised me on the fair price of market goods, found reliable taxi drivers, delivered messages from the neighbors, and warned me to wear boots before I stepped out on a muddy day. Life was better with them as part of our family.

5

Laughter

It wasn't long before my body objected to its new surroundings. Even though I drank bottled water and soaked fresh fruits and vegetables in chlorinated water, I got diarrhea within the first few days—and it didn't go away for a year. I never knew when it would interrupt me.

One evening after work, I volunteered to help sort children's books at a small, foreign-run school. As I combed through dust-caked paperbacks—the state of every object untouched for more than an hour in the desert weather—my stomach gurgled.

I felt embarrassed to ask where to find the bathroom, but I was desperate. The teacher pointed toward the far corner of the backyard and asked her daughter to go with me. With a flashlight, a roll of pink toilet paper, and her four-year-old in tow, I hurried to the outhouse. Inside, I was relieved to see it was not a squatty toilet. The mud and straw room contained a high mound at its center, topped

10

with a white ceramic toilet seat. I barely stripped off my bottom layer in time.

I sat and listened to the voice of the mullah chanting the evening call to prayer from a loudspeaker at a nearby mosque, and chuckled at my odd circumstances. I never would have imagined this would be my life.

My reverie was interrupted by pounding on the door. "I need to go potty! I need to go potty!" pleaded the little girl.

"Um… just a minute," I called back as another wave of diarrhea started. I panicked. Would she push through the door and find me in this condition? Would she soil her pants? How would I explain to her mother why she couldn't get to the toilet in time?

The girl waited longer, and we both walked back to the school in clean clothes. I felt lucky and laughed to myself.

But it wouldn't be often I could find humor in the absurdity or helplessness of my situations. As time went on I lost my sense of humor in the seriousness of life around me. I often wondered how Afghans could laugh in the face of seemingly overwhelming difficulty—laughter seemed a luxury even I couldn't afford. Later I understood it was how they survived. It would be integral to my sustainability, too.

6

Weep with those Who Weep

*When Jesus saw her weeping, and the Jews who
came with her also weeping, he was greatly
disturbed in spirit and deeply moved. He said,
"Where have you laid him?" They said to him,
"Lord, come and see." Jesus began to weep. So
the Jews said, "See how he loved him!"*
—John 11: 33-36, NRSV

Until Afghanistan, no one close to me had ever
died. But for Afghans, living through the death
of someone you knew was as expected as the month of
Ramadan.

Women died in childbirth. Babies died from
malnutrition. Fathers, brothers, and sons died fighting,
and everyone in between was collateral damage. Car
crashes were often fatal, because medical care was too far
away or insufficient.

Deaths caused by everyday hazards, normally
avoidable in developed countries, were even more

surprising. Gas bottle explosions, gas poisoning from heaters, and electrocution claimed lives regularly.

The first time I visited an Afghan home was to mourn the death of a newborn baby. When we arrived, the mother sat in the corner of a back room lit only from the late summer sun creeping around the corner of the hallway. She was wailing, which I later learned is the grieving custom. I stared at her pale skin and bone-thin body, and wondered if she had eaten since her baby died.

My housemate sat down next to the woman on the floor, wrapped her arm around her back, and whispered soothing words I didn't yet understand. I sat next to them and stared at the floor, praying for God's presence to break through the darkness of the house. I left feeling useless. Did I have anything to offer these people?

◆ ◆ ◆

The next summer, I was at the home of one of our kokos, having a traditionally late, relaxed dinner outdoors. By then, I knew enough about Afghan culture and spoke enough Dari to feel comfortable on long visits with my new friends.

Everyone in his large family was there: his sweet aging mother, preteen boys mostly interested in whether I knew any World Wrestling Entertainment wrestlers, and three sons in their twenties, who were so handsome I thought they belonged on the cover of *GQ Magazine*. The older sons' introspection about their country and culture impressed me. I knew they would grow into the kind of adults who could make a difference around them.

A few days after our dinner, a power line broke and

fell into a puddle on the cement patio of their yard. The oldest son walked through the puddle and died instantly.

How I wished I could rewind time to before the accident.

◈ ◈ ◈

There would be more deaths to come. As the years passed, I adjusted, but my sorrow never diminished. I wept with those who wept.

7

Ugly Fruit

Like so much else in Afghanistan, fruit always appeared shabby. It was not genetically modified to grow bigger or look more colorful. Nor was it waxed or preserved. To make it look more appealing, market vendors splashed water on their produce from nearby sewage ditches. Apples and bananas looked the worst, as they bruised in transit from the field to the vendor's cart. Despite the blemished skins, the fruit tasted incredible. Each piece contained the perfect texture, juiciness, and flavor. Getting a good piece of fruit was never a gamble.

The fruit, like the country, was authentic. And it was undeveloped compared to the West. Cities were not planned. Neighborhoods had no building or design codes. Deserts spread, vast and sparse. Mountains towered, magnificent and perilous. It was remote, messy, untamed. The rawness captivated me.

Initially, I encouraged development, but life's simplicity exposed me to a reality that wasn't inferior to my fast-paced Western experience. I grew to prefer not only the fruit, but the quality of relationships and the rhythm of life.

My challenge became making life better through economic development, while upholding the culture and way of life.

8

You Know You're in Afghanistan When

A couple of months after arriving, I took a trip with two new acquaintances. We flew to Herat, one of the largest cities in Afghanistan, near the border of Iran. Our experience at the airport made the trip an event, rather than a quick few-hundred-mile hop.

The ordeal was so long we made up a game titled, "You Know You're in Afghanistan When." Every time something unexpected happened, we completed the phrase YKYIAW.

You know you're in Afghanistan when:

...you arrive at the airport, and although you have a pass to enter the inside drop-off area, the guard still refuses your entry.

... you check in for the flight at the ticket counter, but your name is not on the flight manifest, and handing the agent your original ticket, issued by their airline, means nothing.

… you are escorted down a back hall, to a hidden corner, or behind a curtain and frisked by a female airport employee.

… something—anything—doesn't work. Machines were typically in disrepair and the power was often out.

… the boarding gate area is an outdoor warehouse-like structure. The men and women separate themselves and sit in cheap plastic chairs.

… someone more important than you arrives, displacing you from a place of honor, the boarding area. You are herded to the tarmac where you stand for thirty minutes without an explanation.

… you learn to make the best of every situation. From the tarmac, we were led into another outdoor temporary structure. It was clear to everyone we were not going to be leaving soon. People spread out blankets and turned up the music on their phones. Some local boys showed up to sell bottled water and packaged cookies. We enjoyed the music and bought a snack. Four hours after our arrival we finally boarded our plane.

◆ ◆ ◆

Once in Herat, we dressed like the local women, in a *chadar namaz*. This was a long, black sheet that fit over our head and was pinned under the chin, leaving only our faces exposed. Because I am taller than most women, my sheet did not reach my ankles. I wondered how unfashionable I looked in my mid-calf *chadar namaz*.

We visited the ruins of a walled fortress dating to the time of Genghis Khan. Following our guide, we crawled through the remains of the stairways and rooms. I tried to enjoy the adventure, knowing I was visiting a place most people would never see. But the annoyance of my constricting clothes and the heat diminished my pleasure.

This was much like everyday life in Afghanistan—too uncomfortable to enjoy my experience. The weather was either too hot or too cold. My head scarf slipped off or my pants clung to my legs in the heat. I worried whether I was dressed appropriately, or if my Dari was adequate. I worried if I had accidentally offended someone, and if I would have access to a bathroom when I needed one.

Secretly, I wondered how I was coping in comparison to other foreigners. In my need to be organized, the others seemed more spontaneous. I was sure they reveled in the unpredictable work environment. They probably loved eating new food and wearing different clothes and learning a new language. I tried to convince myself it was fun, but learning basic life skills in a new environment wore me out.

As I began meeting other international Christians, I inquired about different aspects of our lives to gauge their adjustment. To my surprise, I wasn't alone. Different things bothered us, but we all struggled. I found comfort in this, and added another truism to my game: you know you're in Afghanistan when you make real friends.

9

Water: The Great Equalizer

How I missed hot water during the winter. I missed it flowing from a faucet or steaming up a shower. Instead, it froze in our pipes. Every morning, koko drew a bucket of water from a nearby well. I held my breath as I splashed my face with the frigid water, and waited as long as possible to wash my hair.

For many weeks, the public bathhouses were the only place in the city with warm, running water. Since our houses had showers, this was not a place foreigners visited often. But I was desperate. So I asked Aisha to take me. She and her two daughters waited with me in a line for almost two hours. I watched as children grew impatient, then found creative ways to entertain themselves. One family brought a bag of snacks, and when the snacks were eaten, the plastic bag became a kickball.

My frozen pipes brought me together with the rest of

the women in the city, and it was one of the few times I felt equal with them. They talked to me as if I were Afghan.

"Can you hold this for me?"

"How many people are waiting in front of you?

"Have you been here a lot this winter?"

When it was finally our turn, the four of us shared a room with two other women. Two faucets near the ground spewed warm water. I lathered my washcloth with soap.

"No, no," Aisha cut in. First, she poured water over my head from plastic containers. Then she took my arm and scrubbed it with her own coarse cloth, stopping once to show me the layers of dead skin before she rinsed it and moved to my other arm. As she worked on my arms, her daughter washed my back. Satisfied with their work, they dumped another bucket of water over me.

Sitting in a puddle with water dripping off my face, I felt bathed in humility and gratitude. I often thought I had something valuable to teach Afghans. But in the simple act of bathing, I learned how much they could teach me about their resourcefulness. I just had to willingly go to the most common of places and keep my mind open.

10

Questions

The needs in Afghanistan overwhelmed me. In rural areas, people lived on diets that lacked essential nutrients. The educational system was weak in the cities and almost nonexistent outside them. Every normal family grappled with unemployment and debt. The government couldn't fund societal needs, and the hospitals barely met medical needs.

I worked in the agricultural sector. My job, at both the new business and the NGO, took me across five of the north-central provinces. Though I mainly worked in our office, I occasionally traveled with our teams to see our field work. Signs of poverty were everywhere: children in ragged clothes with dirty feet, old women missing teeth, able-bodied men with no work. Despite their meager means, villagers always greeted us with a cup of tea in the shade of a lone tree or tattered shelter.

A sun-dried tomato project was one of my main focuses in those first years. It was close to our office, and a female Afghan colleague and I visited nearby villages, recruiting women to process the tomatoes. Before each visit, we alerted the village elder, who then gathered eligible women and supervised our meeting to ensure we only spoke of employment opportunities and not Western propaganda. Tea was served to guests first. As we waited for the others to receive their cups, we talked among ourselves.

"Hello, how are you, and how is your family? Is everyone well?" I greeted the woman seated next to me. She asked me the same questions.

"Thank God, we are well," we simultaneously answered with the expected pleasantry. Then they moved to more personal questions, which were often, "How did you learn Dari ? Where are you from? Are you married? Do you have children?"

When the greetings finished, my Afghan colleague called everyone's attention to start the meeting. She explained the job requirements and then asked who was interested. The most outgoing women spoke first.

"I am very happy to work with you."

"I don't have anyone to watch my children so I cannot leave my home."

"My mother is sick and there is no one else to take care of her."

"I will surely buy a beautiful scarf with the first day's wage."

We went from village to village, selecting a few women from each, and carrying home the weight of their difficult circumstances.

Some nights, I stayed awake thinking of the people I met. I wondered why God allowed such hardship. And

I wondered how I could help when the problems seemed endless. Did I have the courage to try, however small my impact? What kind of change could I hope for?

Riding from Kabul to Mazar one day, my observation of Afghanistan's cruel realities warred within me. When we reached the heights of the Salang Pass, covered in a thick blanket of snow, the splendor of creation restored me. I could not ask, "God, where are you?" when I was surrounded by this view. Instead, from the back seat, I wrote these words:

Clouds settle between the mountains
Just below where the peaks touch the sky
Looming like my questions, many

In this world of mystery, You hold me tightly
In this world of hardness, You hold me softly

A blue face pressed against a bus window
A doorway dug out from under the snow
A boarded-up shack, a lone gas pump

Trucks heaped with goods strapped on tight
Boys earning their bread at the chain-up
Another day

And the people cry out
Love me, please love me
For I am lovely
See me, please see me
For though I am lowly, I will not be forgotten

11

Opening My Hands and Heart

As graduate students preparing for our fieldwork, we were asked to share what caused us the most anxiety. Many students said they were nervous about culture shock, homesickness, and job performance. I worried about living without chocolate.

I was sure my faithful obedience to God's calling meant sacrifices from the inconvenient to the torturous. I braced myself to give up comfort foods—not the least being chocolate. But a surprising truth about God's goodness and generosity was about to unfold.

Within a week of my arrival, I discovered I could buy Snickers just about anywhere. They might be expired or melted, but they still tasted like chocolate.

As an added blessing, I could receive U.S. mail through the military base thirty minutes away. My mom often sent care packages with Ghirardelli chocolate chips, Starbucks dark chocolate espresso beans, and Oreos, which I squirreled away under my bed, along with locally bought Dr. Pepper. I consumed them in the secrecy of my room so I didn't feel guilty about not sharing with my housemates.

I was still rationing treats when my American friend, Anna, received a care package from home with ingredients to make Southern-style fried chicken. She bought a fresh chicken and came to our house to cook the meal. After we ate our fill, she gave us the leftovers.

"Why don't you want to take the leftovers home?" I asked, baffled. "You'll have dinner prepared for the whole week!"

She frowned. "Why would I want to keep it for myself when I can share with my friends? My enjoyment multiples when I am blessing others with the blessings I have received."

Her answer changed my perspective. I grew up learning to share, and I considered myself kind and generous. But was I willing to risk giving something away that may not be replaced?

After that, I stopped storing things under my bed and shared more. Contrary to the laws of science, my goody box was never empty. The more I gave, the more I received.

◈ ◈ ◈

At the end of my first year in Afghanistan, Anna became ill. The world-renowned specialist caring for her in a nearby German army hospital could not diagnose her. She almost died several times.

I visited her on the weekends. The hospital was

Western style, which reminded me of home. The staff wore Western hospital uniforms, and women did not cover their heads. I appreciated the air conditioning after traveling to the hospital in 100-degree heat.

"My feet are so cold in this air conditioning," Anna said. So, on my next visit, I brought her my new pink, fuzzy socks from a care package. I needed them for the cold winter ahead, but Anna's relief made me forget about the winter. I didn't ask for the socks back, and I never had a shortage of wool socks to keep my feet warm when winter finally came.

Besides opening my hands in generosity, Anna taught me to open my heart to receive from others: their support, their encouragement, their help, their listening ear, their stories, and their love. At first I didn't think I needed any of this. And I didn't want to burden anyone else. But I needed to be part of a community if I was going to survive.

12

_f_ailure

Summer in Mazar, a lower altitude city, was at least six months long and brutally hot. There was little escape from the heat because my clothes needed to cover me fully.

My first full summer was the hardest. My culture shock had peaked. I was encountering my first significant work challenges. And my irritation and exhaustion rose with the temperatures.

USAID funded the start-up costs for our sun-dried tomato project. The grant paid to import basic equipment and buy raw materials from the local market. We recruited women from the surrounding villages to wash, cut, and lay the tomatoes in the sun. The dried tomatoes were hand collected and packaged for sale. It was a simple plan on paper, but problems cropped up at every stage.

I attended periodic meetings at USAID's office to discuss our progress. My time there only contrasted the disparity between their world and mine. They had money to fuel a generator constantly, which meant air conditioned offices. Although the first three minutes offered a welcome relief, it was soon uncomfortably cool and exacerbated the struggle to readjust to the heat.

Meeting with their staff was even less pleasant. The person assigned to our grant was under pressure to give glowing reports to USAID about the positive impact of the projects they funded. But I never had anything positive to report. A drought caused the price of tomatoes to triple. The equipment from Turkey arrived late. Then it got stuck at customs. The obstacles never seemed to disappear.

I kept thinking I would learn to handle these meetings better. I would argue more effectively or have a witty comeback to the unfair expectations. I would convince the grant officer that our obstacles were a normal part of business in a difficult environment. But I didn't.

Toward the end of the summer, it was clear we wouldn't meet our production goal. I broke into a cold sweat as I sat opposite the grant officer ready to give this update.

When I finished, he slammed a stack of manila file folders on his desk.

"Do you know what this is?" he asked. Not waiting for a reply, he continued, "This is a pile of failed projects. Failed, Failed, Failed," he said as he took the top files from the stack, one at a time, and threw them onto a new pile.

"Now you're telling me this pile is where your file belongs too? I expected better from you, Sonora, I really did. You have an MBA after all! So what should I tell my boss? We have a pile of lemons?"

"I guess so." I stammered.

"What kind of an answer is that?" I thought. "Give it to him! Tell him he doesn't know anything about the world beyond his air conditioner. Tell him he can take his money and go home. He doesn't know how hard everyone is working to try to make this a success. All he cares about is looking good so he can take credit for someone else's work."

I left without saying anything more, but his words stayed with me. If our project failed, so had I.

Riding back to the office, I remained silent, but inside I was fuming. With the windows rolled down and the hot air pressing on my face, I tugged my headscarf more tightly around my neck and wondered if it was possible to self-ignite.

By the time I reached home, I feared my anger would last until the first autumn breeze. As I told my housemates about my meeting, I noticed a spider on the wall. I swung my shoe to kill it, which released some pressure, like opening the lid on a boiling pot.

After this, I was more aware of the tension building in my body. When I washed my hair, I scrubbed with an aggression necessary to remove lice. I cracked two fillings from grinding my teeth in my sleep. And one evening while washing dishes, a glass slipped from my soapy fingers and smashed on the floor. The sound felt like an electric shock, destroying my poise. Feeling out of control, I took a deep breath and prayed. I needed to relax, but I didn't know how.

13

The Getaway

*We pray that you'll have the strength to stick it out over
the long haul. Not the grim strength of gritting your
teeth but the glory-strength that God gives. It is strength
that endures the unendurable and spills over into joy,
thanking the Father who makes us strong enough to take
part in everything bright and beautiful that he has for us.*
—Colossians 1:11–12, The Message

An opportunity arose to take a short vacation to
a remote guesthouse in the mountains outside
of Kabul. There it was green, and the air was fresh and
twenty degrees cooler.

I wore my Afghan village attire and left with high
spirits for a relaxing weekend. An Afghan man picked
us up and drove us out of the city. When we turned off
the main road, my friend and I looked at each other with
anticipation. By our watches, it wasn't much further, but a
half hour later we seemed to be in the middle of nowhere.

Another ten minutes passed. Then ten more. My friend and I looked at each other with increasing anxiety.

Suddenly the car stopped. We froze.

"What's going on? I thought. "Have we been tricked and kidnapped by our driver?"

A man appeared from behind some bushes and approached the car to speak to the driver.

"Were they executing their exchange?" I thought back to all the kidnapping stories I'd heard.

"Oh, dear God, should we run?" I thought, just as our driver turned to us.

"This is Koko Aziz," he said. "He'll help you carry your bags to the lodge."

My friend and I exhaled at the same time, as we exchanged a look and shrugged.

Koko made his way around bushes and through streams, carrying both of our bags while we struggled through the terrain empty-handed. After fifteen minutes, a structure came into view—we had arrived.

That afternoon, we ate lunch on a balcony overlooking a crystal-clear brook. A shepherd boy guided a herd of sheep down the mountain and across the water. Women walked beside their heavily packed donkeys down the footpath parallel to the stream. We wondered how far they had traveled and how far they had to go. At sundown, women gathered upstream to collect water in large jars they slung onto their heads to carry home.

At night, we left our windows open and fell asleep to the sound of water. It felt like paradise.

The next morning, we cooled our feet in the stream, and talked about how different our lives were compared to those who lived in such isolation. I reflected over the past year, as I watched the water flow over my toes. Gratitude swelled in my heart. I felt perfectly at peace and exactly where I was supposed to be.

I went home rejuvenated and more positive about the future. However, after one day back in the relentless heat and up against the same obstacles at work, I knew I needed more than a few days of rest.

I started to make changes. Time with God became a priority each morning. I shared my struggles with others. On some weekends, I napped. The changes weren't instant fixes, but as I shifted my habits, I became more aware of God's revitalizing presence.

14

"I"dol

*All who make idols are nothing, and the
things they treasure are worthless...*
—Isaiah 44:9, NIV

"I" is the first letter of idol. That is where my
wrongful worship started.

I went to Afghanistan equipped with a BA in religion,
an MBA, a driver's license, English fluency, computer
competency, and dogged determination. I built myself
into someone who didn't need help. I was just like the
carpenter in Isaiah 44:9–20, who used half his wood to
cook his dinner and the other half to carve an image to
worship.

I looked to my work to sustain me, but found my
credentials useless. Knowing Islamic theology was
not the key to people's hearts. My MBA was critical
to do my job, but it did not make me a successful
businesswoman. My driver's license was immaterial—
women didn't drive in Afghanistan. I needed Dari

fluency, not English fluency, and cultural competency, not computer competency. Here, my determination only wore me out.

When my strengths turned out to be useless, I saw how I had made them into idols. After a few years, I finally learned God did not bring me to Afghanistan for my résumé. He brought me to clear every delusion that I could replace Him.

15

Holy Rest

*By the seventh day God had finished the work he
had been doing; so on the seventh day he rested
from all his work. Then God blessed the seventh
day and made it holy, because on it he rested from
all the work of creating that he had done.*
—Genesis 2:2–3, NIV

I have always enjoyed working. I find an odd pleasure in being occupied. And even greater satisfaction when the occupation turns into accomplishment. In Afghanistan, this was my downfall.

I was used to cramming multiple activities into one day, but when everything took longer at home and at work, it meant I accomplished less. I never anticipated the toll of walking down the road, buying groceries, and cooking a meal. Until I spoke Dari at a conversational level, every day felt like walking uphill against the wind.

My exhaustion aggravated me, but I refused to rest. I kept pushing. I had an agenda—a lofty one. I justified that it was God's agenda, and I wouldn't stop until it was finished.

Scripture, however, told me otherwise. God didn't want me to work myself weary. "It's useless to rise early and go to bed late, and work your worried fingers to the bone. Don't you know he enjoys giving rest to those he loves?" (Psalm127:2, The Message).

God gave me work—good, meaningful work—but He also provided rest. And just as God worked and rested, I was to do the same. Maybe rest was part of God's agenda for me here.

16

God's Love

After almost a year and a half, I flew home for my first visit. My alma mater invited me to speak about international economic development. But I felt inadequate to share any academic, intellectual, or technical insights. When I was a student I listened to guest speakers with decades of experience, not sixteen months.

So, I selected a topic I knew each student would face: suffering. I outlined the different views of suffering from the world's major religions. When I tried to conclude with an application, I got stuck. I felt emotion beyond words, which was evident by the empty page in front of me.

I was unraveling. My thoughts raced. My heart ached. Then nausea swept over me. I paced then sat, bracing my head in my arms. Suffering was tangible now. I couldn't decide which was worse: my sudden illness or emotional upheaval.

In a daze, my mind turned over a conversation with my best friend earlier that day.

"Afghan women have such difficult lives," I explained, giving examples of a few stories I'd heard. "More than anything I want them to know God loves them and they aren't alone. But I am struggling to do this. My Dari is still limited. It's hard to connect with them because of our cultural differences. I keep telling God how important this is, hoping He will give me some wisdom or insight. But I'm not getting any answers."

"Sonora, do you believe God loves you?" she interrupted.

"Of course I do!" I said, agitated.

I lifted my sweaty forehead. There it was—like finding the one broken bulb in a string of Christmas lights. I knew God loved me, but I thought I didn't need God's love as much as other people. Others had worse problems, bigger sins. As I yearned for them to know God's love, I hadn't allowed God to love *me* fully. This kept me from knowing and experiencing Him at a deeper level. It took seeing the suffering and depravity of life in Afghanistan to see my own depravity hidden behind the illusion of my clean and comfortable past.

17

7he Guest House

This being human is a guest house.
Every morning a new arrival.

A joy, a depression, a meanness...

Welcome and entertain them all!
Even if they're a crowd of sorrows,
who violently sweep your house
empty of its furniture,
still, treat each guest honorably.

—Mewlana Jalaluddin Rumi

As Rumi encouraged in his poem "The Guest House," I considered how to welcome every visitor into my home. Greeting pain and discouragement with a cup of tea wasn't natural to me. I preferred to stay behind a locked door. But that was not the Afghan way. So, I kept the door open, and realized suffering is accompanied by a surprising escort: the Trinity.

In opening my heart to greet suffering, I realized I also let in a Suffering Savior, a Constant Comforter, and a Loving Father. God wanted to come live inside all the parts of my life, and meet me especially in the ugliest. God did not fear pain as I did. God confronted and conquered it. God did not insist I have a quick drink with suffering and show it the door. Instead, He got out the bath towel and pillow mint, and showed suffering to my favorite room where comfort and safety lived.

God's goodness did not abolish suffering from earth. God's goodness moved beyond human solutions and came as Emmanuel: God with us. He came into the suffering and experienced it firsthand—and severely. He defeated death and pain and brought us abundant life, making a way for us to enjoy life even while the suffering on earth continues. While I yearn for the time when there are no tears or pain, Jesus's resurrection allows me to enjoy God's Kingdom on earth.

God's presence in my life is an assurance I have someone mightier than anything in this world. His presence means I can meet life with the laughter of fearless living, because God is the giver of impossible gifts. The birth of Isaac (which means "he laughs") to aged parents was a sign of God's surprising way of fulfilling His promise of blessing, which his parents were incapable of accomplishing in their own power. I can free fall into the arms of the One whose immeasurable love delivers me from suffering without hope.

18

Stille Nacht

I experienced many moments when I felt I was made and purposed to be in Afghanistan. They felt as familiar as hearing music and knowing the words to the song.

I often felt that purpose when I was in the middle of a normal, mundane task. The feeling washed over me without warning. But a few experiences, like my second Christmas in Afghanistan, uniquely stood out.

I was invited to join two international families in a Christmas play at the German army base. The play ended with a flute duet of *Stille Nacht* (Silent Night) played by the oldest child and myself.

I felt a flicker of nerves in my stomach as I looked out to the several hundred soldiers in the audience. We stepped on stage and played the first line, our harmony breaking the silence that had fallen across the room. On the second line, a few reverent voices joined us, and by the third line, everyone in the room sang *Stille Nacht* in unison. I felt God's presence as German soldiers sang the familiar tune in a language unfamiliar to me. I was thankful the music was simple, because I lost concentration on my playing, and entered the sacredness of the moment. It felt like heaven reached down.

Afterward many of the soldiers thanked me and told me the evening "made my Christmas." It made my Christmas too. It made my whole year. All the struggles just to live: the heat, the cold, the agony of learning Dari, the lack of achievement in my job, the culture shock. Everything difficult faded in the reassurance that God brought me here for something bigger than myself.

19

The Darkest Parts of Us

In Afghanistan, stories didn't need the internet to travel thousands of miles in minutes. The rumor mill never shut down. The stories I heard from women were often so remarkable they didn't seem real. They reminded me of Old Testament stories, full of the darkest parts of humanity: murder, incest, betrayal, and injustice.

A poor family with two teenage girls lived in a village about an hour away from me. The parents went to another town to find work, and left the girls with their uncle in the city. The uncle drugged and impregnated both girls. When they returned home to their parents and could no longer hide their condition, their father was furious. He questioned his daughters about their activities in the city, but they gave no explanation. Out of shame, he tried to shoot his daughters. Their mother was shot when she put herself in the line of fire. One daughter was injured, and the other jumped over the courtyard wall and found refuge with neighbors. Eventually, the truth was uncovered, but not before the uncle fled his home, never to be seen again.

This story disturbed me. What kind of man could do such a thing to his nieces? But evil infiltrates every society, not just Afghanistan. Sin is not contained by political or ethnic boundaries.

What kind of father could shoot his own child? To an Afghan, the answer was, "the right kind." A father who would do anything to protect the honor of his family was exemplary. He was guided by his cultural values—as we all are.

It's easy to judge Afghans or anyone throughout history. But what God taught me from the Old Testament—and from the Old Testament-like stories I heard in Afghanistan—was not to look in and condemn, but to examine myself for the same rebellion in my own dark heart.

20

Θospitality and Θostility

*A*fghans are known for both their hospitality and fierce defense of their nation—an odd and delicate combination[1]. And they are proud of this reputation.

For Afghans, there are two kinds of outsiders: the peaceful passersby and the threatening invaders. Foreigners may fall into either category, depending on their intention. A respectful guest is greeted with world-class hospitality. But an aggressor toward the Afghan way of life—its power structures, culture, or worldview—is not welcome.

External forces threaten Afghanistan in violent and nonviolent ways. Afghans are prepared to meet both with any response necessary. They don't want to take orders from outsiders; they want self-determination. Even societal change is best initiated from within.

---

[1] Here, the term "Afghan" is used to name the population living within the political boundaries of current-day Afghanistan. Afghans are an ethnically diverse people, and to group them all together is an overgeneralization. In this book, though, the term will be used for simplicity.

I was welcomed as an honored guest. Afghans did not see me as a threat. By wearing conservative clothes that respected their culture, I communicated I wasn't there to challenge their values. By learning their language, I communicated I wanted to be part of their tradition.

My welcome was not a passive acceptance. I was actively embraced. People invited me to their homes from the beginning, and the invitations never stopped. The first time I visited the home of a koko, his wife said, "While you are here you will miss your family, so you must come and visit us. We are your family now."

Other times invitations weren't necessary. Afghans celebrated their major religious holidays by visiting friends, neighbors, and family over three-day periods. Attendance was presumed. Even strangers were greeted with kindness. Guests could stay for days, even weeks, and the hosts never asked them to leave.

The work of hosting fell to the women, who cooked, cleaned, and raised children. As much as I heard women complain, I also saw how important community was to them. Behind the walls that physically divided one family from the next was a group of people who relied on one another. I grew to appreciate their interconnectedness.

21

ℱreedom

Light, space, zest—that's God!
—Psalm 27:1, The Message

When I got the balance of the bat synchronized with the bounce of the ball, I found out how much I enjoyed backyard cricket. Hitting a ball over the mud wall into the neighbor's yard yielded a certain satisfaction, as did running back and forth between wickets, shouting, laughing, and clapping.

It was rare to find a private space for sports in Mazar. The yard was filled with dirt, rocks, potholes, and thorn patches. We didn't have the proper equipment, but a worn tennis ball and plastic yard chairs sufficed. With some imagination and a loose interpretation of the rules, a few international families created an environment where men and women could play together, away from the restrictions of the local culture. The freedom I had in those few hours made me yearn for more, and brought back memories of a past full of space to explore without any walls inhibiting me.

Growing up, my brothers and I played in a summer community baseball league. As I got older, I played basketball, softball, and tennis. Our rectangular front yard was a touch-football field and the backyard, a wiffle-ball field. Our paved driveway had a basketball hoop. Our homemade, wooden play gym turned into an American Gladiators arena when we got out our arsenal of Nerf guns. There was a hill for sledding in the winter and a small willow tree for climbing in the summer. A big oak tree hosted a tire swing. We spent countless hours in the woods hiking, building forts, making paths, and digging for critters. After dark, we played hide-and-go-seek with a flashlight and caught fireflies. Other nights we made a bonfire and roasted marshmallows.

All these activities included the neighborhood kids, mostly boys. Playing and learning at home and school was an important part of my childhood.

Life for children in Afghanistan was so different. Here, public schools were in shambles, there were no community organizations, and no resources or space for recreation. At school, boys and girls separated, beginning the divide between the sexes.

This was especially obvious when my foreign coworkers and I spent a night at a local home. Our hosts were three adult brothers, living on the same property with their wives and children. The land was divided by mud-wall partitions that did more to separate men and women than the individual family units. The men lived on the front of the land, because it was closest to the road, and therefore, the public. The women's area contained an outdoor space for cooking and a room where they slept, dressed in head coverings.

The family had a farm property down the road from the house. As guests, we were invited to see it. When we returned home, the women had prepared the evening meal, and we separated from the men to eat.

"How did you like the farm?" the women asked.

"It was very nice," we all agreed.

"What was it like?" they wondered.

It was only a five-minute walk from their house, but they had never seen it. I ached at having the privilege to do something they could not. I saw how free I was in every way, despite often feeling otherwise.

I was free not just because I grew up in a different culture, but because knowing God made me free. The rules I lived by as a woman in Afghanistan were not easy. They almost broke me. But they could not deprive me of my value as a person created in the image of God. They could not take away my personality. They could not invalidate my salvation. No confines of human law could separate me from the freedom of living in right relationship with God.

22

My Worlds Colliding

"Isn't it time your dad visited you?" asked the founder of my organization. He was planning his semi-annual visit and thought he should bring my dad. I was surprised when my dad accepted the invitation.

My dad is a pretty cool guy, and I was glad he was coming, but I worried about him. I wondered how he would react to the disorder and unpredictability of life in Mazar. How would he feel surrounded by a language and culture he didn't know? Would he get ill from eating new foods?

"It will be hot, but don't pack shorts," I reminded him. My list of instructions grew longer. "Bring shoes you can easily slip in and out of at people's homes. Don't look at or speak to Afghan women on the street. And since it's a busy season for me at work, you may want to bring a book in case you have down time."

Curious Afghan friends and colleagues asked about my dad's profession. Since he is a pastor, I had to think for a moment before choosing to be honest.

"My dad is like a mullah for Christians."

"He is a much respected man," they said. I felt relieved by this response. "We will show him his due respect."

Every day, my dad came to my office carrying a copy of Jack London's *Call of the Wild*, his childhood favorite. But my Afghan colleagues were so eager to show him our work that he didn't have time to read it.

"With your permission, we would like to take your father to our university and show him the new science lab."

"With your permission, we would like to take your father to our research farm."

"With your permission, we would like to give your father a tour of the nearby ancient city."

Thus began my dad's introduction to Afghan hospitality. In their eyes, there was no barrier in welcoming my Christian father. And my dad encountered no walls as he engaged in every activity.

Dad took more pictures in a week than I had taken in three years. He snapped photos of an abandoned Russian tank on the grounds of a famous old palace. When we passed a de-mining crew combing the roadside hill for active mines, he took more photos. When our driver insisted, my dad visited his house and took pictures of his spectacular garden of roses, apples, and pomegranates.

As we returned to the outskirts of Mazar, my dad took a photo of a soldier on duty at the reentry checkpoint. I was sleeping in the backseat and woke to the sounds of an argument. In my many instructions, I forgot to tell my dad not to take photos at any checkpoint.

The soldier was not happy.

"Show me your passports," he demanded in Dari.

"Our passports are at home in Mazar." I said.

"Then give me your camera," he said, extending his arm toward my dad. I didn't want my dad to lose his photos.

"This man is a visitor in your country," I said, "and taking his camera is not a hospitable thing to do. But we can delete your picture."

We showed the picture to the guard, who beamed when he saw his own image. He changed his mind and commanded me to print multiple copies of the photo before I deleted it—an impractical solution. I needed to be more assertive.

I knew, as a foreign woman, I could speak to him as if I were a man. Men raised their voices at each other without creating any ill will between them. I also sensed the soldier was far more interested in meeting a foreign woman, who spoke Dari, than offended by having his picture taken.

So we argued loudly in Dari. My dad looked on, baffled and sheepish. Our driver sat silent, a smile creeping to his lips; he was enjoying the show. Finally, the soldier and I agreed to simply delete the photo and we drove off.

◈ ◈ ◈

Dad felt more relaxed visiting Afghans in their homes. At Aisha's home, he barely waited for the meal to be cleared before he began a soccer game with the boys.

"Goal!" my father yelled, as the three-year-old kicked the ball between the empty plastic Coke bottles my dad set up in the open doorway. I glanced at Aisha and her husband to see if they were amused that my father turned the dinner table—a cloth laid out on the floor—into a soccer field, but they didn't seem to mind.

Before we left, Aisha's husband gave my dad a long, green coat, traditionally worn by leaders. It was an act of honor. Dad accepted the gift with thanks, though he didn't yet understand its significance.

◆ ◆ ◆

I felt nervous taking my dad to visit my friends Zainab and Zahra. They, as a widow and teenage girl, had no man of the house to welcome an adult male visitor.

"Don't worry," they assured me. "We have already told our neighbors your father is coming, so rumors will not start."

They provided a spread of food well beyond their financial means. Tea and bread was a typical meal for them, but for my father they presented a feast of rice, meat, vegetables, and fruit. This was their way to honor him.

Although I had already shared Zainab and Zahra's story with my parents, dad asked them about their lives. In Dari and faltering English, they relived the time the Taliban came in the very room we were seated. They beat Zainab's husband, because he refused to tell them where his son was hidden. Zainab and her husband did not have a son, but the Taliban didn't believe him. He eventually died from his injuries.

"You are smart, daughter. Go to school," Zainab's husband encouraged Zahra before he died. "Perhaps become a doctor so you can help people."

Without a husband and a father, Zainab and Zahra plunged further down the social rung. He was their last surviving male relative. Life grew more difficult. By God's grace, Zainab found a job cleaning at an American family's house.

Before we left their home, the women asked my dad to pray for them, "because you are a big man, close to God."

◆ ◆ ◆

After my dad's departure, my Afghan colleagues told me what a good man he was, "a very devoted mullah for Christians."

"Why do you say that?" I asked.

"Because he carried your Book with him wherever he went."

Without the dust jacket, the Jack London novel resembled a Bible. I never explained otherwise.

I was grateful for my dad's visit. He experienced the acceptance, generosity, and courage of my Afghan friends. Even the mistaken Bible was not met with suspicion or rejection. Dad carried home the real picture of the Afghan people.

23

Experiencing God

Let us know, let us press on to know the Lord;
his appearing is as sure as the dawn;
he will come to us like the showers,
like the spring rains that water the earth.
—Hosea 6:3, NRSV

In my Intro to Bible class my freshman year of college, I learned Christians believe God reveals Himself through tradition, reason, scripture, and experience. Throughout my life, my Christian education focused on the first three concepts—important foundations for navigating a complex world. And along the way, I experienced God, building a faith not ultimately grounded in theology, but in my experience of God. Knowing God allowed me to hear His voice directing my life.

In Afghanistan, I experienced God in the best and worst times, and all the places in between. Most significantly, I experienced Him in the day-to-day drudgery. God was in the bland beans and bitter tea, dusty dreariness and muddy boots. It wasn't because the everyday was the easiest place to experience God—it was because it was the hardest. I searched for Him, cried to Him, pleaded to be near Him. I *needed* Him.

As surely as the dawn and the spring rain, He appeared to me. Were it not for God's faithful, refreshing presence, I could not have endured the challenge of finding purpose in the ordinary days.

24

A Change Inside of Me

I couldn't believe my bad luck. Our business relationship with USAID ended, as did my working relationship with the man who had made my work so miserable, branding me a failure. But when my organization applied for a loan from another donor, he turned out to be our loan officer.

There weren't many foreigners in town, so by this point I had spent plenty of time with him both socially and professionally. I didn't enjoy his company in either environment. One evening, he invited me to dinner. No one else was available to join and make the company more palatable, so I prepared for an unpleasant evening.

We met at a British restaurant, one of the few hangouts for foreigners in Mazar. That night, the restaurant was nearly empty and the service quick. By the time our food arrived, we had finished our small talk. He then revealed why he asked me to dinner. A foreign woman he knew in another part of the country had been kidnapped two weeks ago, and her chances of being found alive didn't look good. He was worried and needed someone to talk to, but struggled to communicate. He stared at his plate, poking the steamed vegetables, which were now cold. I didn't know what to say.

"I'm so sorry," I said, finally breaking our silence.

I had never seen him like this—he actually cared about someone. My animosity turned to pity. There was more to him than a man behind a desk with manila files.

"How do you do it?" he asked, interrupting my thoughts.

"Do what?" I asked.

"How do you do what you do? Why are you the way you are?"

"I really don't know what you mean." I felt truly perplexed by his line of questioning.

"Well, you work in Afghanistan without a salary. You live in a simple house. You don't go on vacations like other expats, and you don't go to their parties."

I paused and prayed. I felt more comfortable living out my faith than talking about it.

"I believe God is real," I said. "I read the Bible and I try to live the way it tells me to."

I braced for an argument, but instead of our typical exchange, he turned back to poking his vegetables. The shift caught me off guard, and we slipped back into silence, as I gave him space to ponder.

Over the years, he turned up in other places. I knew it wasn't coincidence. God was teaching me to love everyone I met in Afghanistan, not just Afghans—to Him, there was no distinction. After that evening, I sought out foreigners who were not Christians, to listen to them and love them. Nothing miraculous happened, except a change inside of me.

25

Tea Time

I was told drinking tea is the cornerstone of Afghan hospitality. But I doubted I would find much time for tea breaks—I was going to Afghanistan to do something important, lasting, and meaningful.

I was wrong about the tea. I couldn't avoid it, nor the brownish stain it left on my teeth.

During my first few years abroad, the thought of drinking tea and making conversation with Afghan women felt intimidating, so I never visited a home alone. One or two other foreign women, who spoke Dari, always accompanied me. I discovered it wasn't important for us to say much. The Afghan women needed someone to listen to them, and didn't mind that I couldn't understand all of what they said. In their culture, drinking tea with other women was their emotional outlet.

So I listened. As the years passed, my Dari comprehension increased, along with my understanding of normal life for Afghan women.

"My husband's brother's family finally left after two weeks. Today I won't cook a meal!"

"I have wonderful news. My niece, who had been kidnapped, has been found. It was the neighbor's son who took her. They went to Pakistan and got married. Now the families will have a big party. Tomorrow I will go shopping with my sisters for pretty dresses."

"It has been sunny all week, so I was able to wash all of my family's clothing just in time. We had nothing clean left to wear."

"We just came back from Kabul. My brother's son was in a car accident and we were taking care of him in the hospital."

"After this baby is born, no more babies."

I grew to cherish the hours talking over tea. Eventually I realized that building relationships with these women was the most meaningful thing I did. Their friendship enriched my life. Their tenacity grew my courage. And their circumstances put my world in perspective.

◆ ◆ ◆

Getting to know God was like getting to know Afghan women. I needed to stop doing stuff for God, and sit with Him. If I wanted to know God better, I had some serious tea drinking to do.

At first, I thought I needed to hold a conversation with God. But like Afghan women, God just wanted me to show up—to listen. Learning His language and tuning my ears to His voice was not too different from learning Dari. It took time and practice.

After three years in Afghanistan, I arrived at a

juncture. I had finished eighteen months of counseling via Skype, to understand myself better and make healthy changes in my habits so I could stay in Afghanistan longer. I left the NGO to focus on our business with a growing team of nationals, moved to a small mud house where I lived alone, re-adjusted my Dari study schedule, and cleared most of my evenings to spend time with God.

◈ ◈ ◈

It was winter, and darkness fell by the time I got home from work. I lit the wood stove, removed my heavy outer layers of clothes, and lay on the floor staring at the ceiling, waiting to hear something from God. Most of the time He was silent. I was tempted to fill the quiet space, but resisted, because I felt meaning in the stillness. It reminded me of Kathleen Norris's words in her book *Dakota*, "Silence is the best response to mystery."

Everything about my life in Afghanistan felt like a mystery. I practiced listening to God that winter, but nothing happened. I didn't sense God telling me anything. But I felt released from the pressure to perform for God. I felt peace in letting go of my need to achieve. I felt centered. I no longer feared if things fell apart, because I knew God was holding me together.

26

Grieving an Identity Lost

By summer 2011, I was confident in my decision to leave Afghanistan. But that didn't make leaving—or coming home—easier.

When I got home to Colorado I drove 10,000 miles around the western half of the United States, visiting friends and family. Between stops, I relished the wide-open spaces. There were no walls, no checkpoints, and no bomb threats. But when I returned home, I still felt an uneasiness I couldn't identify.

I went to see my counselor. At our first session, she asked me to close my eyes and imagine myself walking down the street I lived on in Mazar. Tears streamed down my face, and I pursed my lips to keep composed.

"What are you thinking about?" she asked.

"I'm not thinking about anything. I'm just walking down the street, but my heart hurts. It hurts really bad."

"I think you are grieving," she said. "Could that be possible?"

"No one died," I paused. "I mean, yes, people died,

and some of them I knew. But I am not grieving anyone's death."

"Perhaps you are grieving the loss of your identity—your life in Afghanistan? That is a legitimate loss, just like any other kind of loss."

I tried to voice a rebuttal. But every objection squelched in my mind before it reached my lips. I knew she was right.

"Well, I think we know what we'll be talking about," she said.

We discussed the cycles of grief, which I learned about years earlier when I volunteered at a grief camp for kids whose family members had died. There we decorated clay pots then smashed and glued them back together. The pot symbolized their lives: broken, yet not beyond restoration. At the time, I didn't identify with the object lesson. But now it represented exactly how I felt coming home from Afghanistan. I felt like my heart had shattered and needed to be glued back together.

No one seemed to understand what I was going through. Friends and family expected me to join them in rejoicing about my return. They thought I had gotten my life back. I felt like I had lost it. They were thankful I had come home alive. I was experiencing survivor's guilt. They wanted to pick up where we left off four years ago, but I was different now.

Going through the stages of grief took time. I didn't leave the house much, even for my daily exercise.

By Thanksgiving, I felt normal enough to enjoy the holiday season, and began looking for a new job overseas. I didn't feel passionate about the opportunities, but I needed to move forward. I hoped the spark would reignite, but Afghanistan was the only prospect that excited me. I kept in touch with Zainab, Zahra, and Aisha on Skype. My mother said that was the only time she heard life in my voice.

27

It's Afghanistan

In March 2012, I flew to a recruitment week in Europe for a finance position, in Africa, with an international NGO. But I still felt no spark. During one session about the history of the NGO, my attention faded, and the words "It's Afghanistan" impressed on my mind. After waiting for direction from God for nine months, I knew He was speaking to me. I was thankful.

And then I worried.

I knew my parents would not like this. In fact, I didn't think anyone would be pleased to hear this news—especially the organization recruiting me. Before going home, I informed them I was no longer interested in the position. Several days after I returned home, they called me.

"A finance manager position in Afghanistan unexpectedly opened up yesterday. We'd like to offer it to you. How soon can you start?" I almost fell off my chair.

"I'll take it! I can be there in three days."

That night I shared my decision with my parents.

"It's Afghanistan," I announced, and explained how I had sensed God's direction. After a few moments of tears we prayed and they gave me their blessing.

It didn't take long to adjust to the idea of returning to Afghanistan. I missed Afghans and their way of life. I missed who I was when I was with them. And knowing God more deeply, I knew I was as prepared as I could be.

28

Beginning Again

Returning to Afghanistan was both new and old. This time, I didn't imagine the opening scene of an adventure movie. Everything was exactly as I expected. When I landed in Kabul, I walked confidently to the parking lot and met my Canadian supervisor and our driver.

"*Salaam Alekum*," I greeted them, cheerfully.

"Oh, you speak Dari?" the driver asked.

"Yes, I am from Mazar-I-Sharif." I wanted to see his reaction.

"Are you Afghan?" he said, his polite way of asking my nationality.

"No, I am American, but I lived in Mazar and learned Dari there."

"Very good, very good," he said.

As we sat in Kabul's rush-hour traffic, the driver told me about his life. He had several young children and recently remarried after his first wife died during childbirth the previous year.

The half hour car ride cemented our relationship. He would protect me as his own daughter, and I would serve as his link to information from the worlds outside.

"*Khush amaden*," (welcome) he said as we pulled into the compound where I would live and work. He introduced me to my new coworkers as The Girl from Mazar—a name which stuck until the day I left.

Despite making my first friend, I didn't feel at home. My old friends and colleagues lived hundreds of miles away in Mazar, and everything was new—my city, my office, my colleagues. I was starting over.

I woke early the next morning to the cacophony of mullahs' voices chanting the call to prayer from the mosques encircling my home—a familiar sound that took a few moments to register. Then a terrible loneliness hit me. I took deep breaths to calm myself. I prayed for God to open my heart again to help me love people, and open my hands again to give and receive from them. Then I fell back to sleep. When I woke up, I set about making my next chapter a great one.

29

Predictably Unpredictable

My familiarity with Afghanistan prepared me to expect the unexpected. One week after arriving in Kabul, Zainab called.

"I'm on a bus on my way to Kabul," she said. She couldn't wait any longer to see me. When she arrived I greeted her with a glad heart and a cup of tea in each hand. We talked until the sun began to set. My director found me in the hallway just as Zainab and I were saying goodbye.

"Can you come with me?" she asked.

"Yes, of course." I said. My concern built and my stomach knotted.

I joined her for a Skype call that confirmed several of our colleagues had been kidnapped that afternoon in a rural area where we worked.

"What can I do?" I asked.

"Start praying."

We summoned our other international colleagues from a nearby restaurant, and immediately formed a crisis management team. My role was to prepare a comprehensive physical and mental care plan for our team members, should they be recovered. I gathered contacts from old friends and colleagues, and my new teammates. I created several contingency plans for hospital care and psychological debriefings. We closed our office for the next eleven days, as we prepared for every possible outcome, prayed, ate, and slept.

Those days of waiting felt strange. I couldn't think about what my kidnapped colleagues were facing, so I focused on myself. I wondered if the job I had just begun would end almost before it started. I wondered whether I should look for another job—the chance of my new organization closing was real.

I felt guilty for thinking of myself. I was in a better situation than everyone else involved. I didn't know the victims, so I was not emotionally attached. I wasn't in captivity. I wasn't in charge of leading the crisis management team. And I certainly wasn't responsible for the outcome.

I pictured myself as the smallest two-seater vessel in the game Battleship—the one that is the hardest to find on your opponent's seaboard. Afghanistan was a seaboard of dangerous waters. The bombs went off all around me, but never hit me. Year after year, someone else died, someone else lost a loved one.

The morning we learned our colleagues were rescued, we exhaled a collective sigh. Beyond our immediate relief, we struggled to express our emotions. We had been so careful not to hope. Now we were unsure how to feel.

Eventually some people moved on to other jobs and others, like me, stayed.

30

The Gift

The rest of the summer was unusual. The office reopened, but programming stayed suspended in the region of the kidnapping. The mood of the office shifted; work was slow and the remaining donor reporting deadlines didn't feel as urgent.

The international staff assigned to our field sites to implement safe water, hygiene, and nutrition projects were stranded in Kabul, so we made the most of it. Kabul provided more recreation for internationals than Mazar. My colleagues introduced me to their friends. There was a wider range of restaurants to visit, a tennis court, squash court, and swimming pool. In the basement of our compound, we spread a large mat and projected exercise videos on the wall. During the 2012 summer Olympics, we created our own games. In the evenings, we relaxed on the balcony and played cards.

This season was a gift—full of fun, sheltered from the country's harsh realities. I thought back to the incident in the outhouse five years ago. It was the last time I remembered feeling so lighthearted. Finally, I was laughing again. It felt wonderful.

31

My Hero

One of the many differences in working for my new organization was a rest and relaxation policy. Every eight weeks, we received an allowance to fly outside the country for at least a week. For my first R&R, I planned to go to the United States for my brother's wedding. But I was still waiting for my work permit and multiple-entry visa to be approved before I could leave the country.

Our human resources officer, Masuma, was in charge of getting work permits and visas for our organization's international staff. Her work was excellent, but there were never any guarantees with the Afghan government. In the weeks leading up to the trip, my approval was delayed.

The day I flew out of Kabul, the ministry informed Masuma we could pick up my passport and visa at 2:00 pm. My flight departed at 5:00 pm. We left the office just after 1:00 pm to cross town. As we approached the city center, traffic slowed to a stop. Our driver asked a nearby policeman about the source of the problem.

"There's a demonstration a few streets over. Everything is blocked," shouted the policeman over the traffic.

After thirty minutes, we still hadn't moved. At this rate, if I stayed in the car, I would miss my flight. Our office had a security policy stating internationals were not allowed to walk on the streets. I called my supervisor and asked for an exception.

"No exceptions to the security policy," he said, curtly.

"Sonora, I can do it," Masuma said. "I can get out of the car, walk until I find a taxi, go to the passport office to pick up your documents, and meet you at the airport."

It was my only chance to make my flight.

Traffic finally gave way and we proceeded to Kabul International Airport, arriving just after 3:00 pm. Masuma greeted me at the entrance with my passport and visa. I could hardly believe it.

Masuma was already a hero in my mind. She defied the boundaries society placed on her and followed her dreams. At twenty-two years old she finished her college education and was fluent in English. She worked full time at an NGO while in school, and we hired her after she graduated. She faced intimidating government employees with confidence and professionalism. At home, she tutored her younger brothers and sisters, because the public school's standards were too low, in her opinion. As the oldest girl, she also helped her mother with the cooking and cleaning for their large family.

"Do you ever sleep?" I asked her one day.

"Not very often," she said, as she giggled.

"All of this, and she is so happy," I thought.

Masuma was also hopeful. She was applying

for scholarships to Master's programs abroad, and wasn't dissuaded at the first few rejections. With her determination, I knew she would get an acceptance letter eventually. But that didn't mean she would be allowed to go.

"Don't your parents want you to stay here and get married?" I asked her.

"Of course they want me to get married. But they know I want to accomplish myself first. I already refused the marriage invitation of my cousin. This created problems in my family, but my father supported my decision."

"It sounds like your father is different than many Afghan men."

"Oh yes, my father is not the problem. It's my mother! She still thinks women belong in the home. But my father has always had bigger dreams for me."

I thought about Masuma and the many young women like her, who could positively impact the future of Afghanistan. Would they stay, or choose a better life somewhere else? While I hoped they would stay, I didn't fault them for leaving.

32

Grace for the Tortoise

When I returned from my trip home, I was ready to get back into a routine and start language study. Nasrullah, my new Dari teacher, conveniently lived in my neighborhood. He didn't mind stopping by my office on his way home from work to spend an hour with me a couple times a week. And the extra income helped pay for his sister's college tuition.

Our first weeks together were rough, as he assessed my knowledge and learning style. Having a male teacher opened a new realm of vocabulary. Whereas conversations with Aisha revolved around the home—family relationships, cooking, clothing—Nasrullah talked politics and economics. I felt intimidated by how much I still had to learn.

Nasrullah taught me how to read and write Dari. It was a natural next step as I added more formal words to my vocabulary, and long overdue. I hadn't had the energy for it when I lived in Mazar. I started with a kindergarten primer and a notebook, first writing my ABCs, then strings of letters to form simple words, and finally sentences. I learned vowel sounds and the rules of word and sentence structure. I copied all of this over and over.

"Your handwriting looks like a child's," Nasrullah said, as he reviewed my work.

"I only have a kindergarten reading level, what did you expect?" I joked. I agreed it did not look very professional.

"Still, you are an adult and you want your writing to be taken seriously. Make the letters smaller by tightening up the curves here," he pointed, "and here."

Learning to write from right to left required me to think in a new way—couldn't he cut me some slack? Even during my dictation tests, he didn't allow me more time than I would have received in a formal class. But I benefitted from his strictness.

"Sonora, some day you will thank me," he said with a smile.

Aisha was happy to hear I was learning to read and write. She confessed when she began teaching me five years ago, I was always behind the other two students, and she didn't think I would succeed. Though my homework was accurate, I struggled to think on my feet during lessons. I took a long time to answer questions and I talked slowly. In the end, I surpassed my classmates and became one of her most advanced students. My steadiness outweighed my lack of natural ability. This reminded me of the story of the tortoise and the hare. Maybe the hare crossed the finish line (a conversational level) sooner than I did, but I eventually got there too.

I never enjoyed learning Dari. I liked my teachers; I liked the feeling of improving. But I had to force myself just to attend lessons, and then to study and practice outside of them. It was the Afghans who motivated me. When I made a mistake they didn't laugh at me. If I asked them to repeat a sentence they didn't lose their patience. They appreciated my efforts to learn their language, and always extended grace to this language-bumbling tortoise.

33

Living in the Incongruent

As summer drew to an early close in Kabul, and a steady drizzle cleared the dust in the air, the city lay at rest, as though releasing its problems. But as the rain continued, the mud accumulated, and the respite dissolved as a new problem arose: navigating unpaved roads, now thick with mud and giant puddles.

Rain was both a blessing and a curse, and it reflected the reality of life in Afghanistan. A day could hold both deep joy and sorrow. One moment I was talking with my international colleague about his trip to Thailand, and the next, I was sitting in a Dari lesson with sample sentences like, "Years of foreign wars have flattened Kabul. Countless families have lost their members to war."

During this time, Zainab and Zahra's lives took a turn. Zahra's life was threatened and they needed to disappear quickly. Zahra traveled to Kabul to find a new place to live. Nothing made me as happy as her smile after we'd been apart. And nothing broke my heart more than her tears. She cried one minute then laughed the next, as we watched a video from my farewell party in Mazar the previous year.

Life was often chaotic for Afghans. And whenever I entered their lives, I wanted to help solve their problems. This impulse was tempered by understanding they were accustomed to problems without immediate solutions, and I didn't have the power or resources to fix them. Still, I helped how I could.

Afghans relied on personal connections instead of a formal justice system or public services. So, I called someone I knew who I thought could help Zainab and Zahra. It was a dead end. I continued to keep in close contact with them and realized being a part of their lives was all they needed from me.

34

The Real Savior

"It's a good thing you came tonight. Otherwise we would have been crying ourselves to sleep. Now we are laughing, because you are here. We haven't forgotten our problems, but while you are here we won't worry about them."

Zainab and Zahra now lived in the Kabul area. I kissed them each on opposite cheeks three times, as was customary, and embraced each one—my American addition to our greeting. Sidestepping the wet areas on their carpet, I found my seat on a thin floor cushion. It was nearly as cold inside their mud home as the winter weather. I tried to hide a shiver as I peered at the opposite wall and floor, soaked with melting snow from the roof. Water had taken over half of the room—their only room.

I brought a liter of Coca Cola, three Afghan burgers (grilled chicken, French fries, shredded cabbage, and sliced boiled eggs wrapped in flatbread), chocolate donuts from Kabul's French bakery, and an extra fleece jacket. In Afghanistan, if the guest brought the meal, it would offend the host. But my friends were accustomed to my strange behavior, and I knew they wouldn't take offense. While Zainab scuttled to light the wood stove for tea, Zahra rattled off the latest news.

"Since the shallow well we normally use has frozen, the neighbor man is bringing us buckets of water from the bigger well at the end of the street. But it has been three days since he last came."

A limited supply of water meant their dishes sat unwashed, so they didn't have anything clean to cook in or serve a meal. I didn't know about their water shortage, or their leaking roof, even though I talked with them several times over the phone since my last visit. In those conversations, we talked about the death threats Zahra kept receiving.

I sent up a prayer, "Oh Lord, how much? How long?"

Zahra loves chocolate, so I opened the donuts, hoping to bring instant—albeit temporary—relief. Zainab joined Zahra—the two so engrossed in their tales of the past week they forgot their dinner. Not only were they out of water, but the landlord threatened to kick them out if they didn't increase their rent payment.

No matter how much I listened, or how much I helped them financially, I still felt helpless. I'd never wanted to help anyone as much as these two women. If God loved these women—even more than I—why did He allow such tragedy, abuse, and abandonment in their lives? It was there, in the wickedness of life, that I understood what I needed was not answers, but to follow the longing to know God more, and to feel dissatisfied with anything less. God, and my relationship with Him, was the answer. He didn't send me to take away every pain and fear my friends held in their hearts. But I believe God used me to help them experience His love through me.

This was my new prayer for my friends—that having exhausted all human deliverance, they would fall into the secure and loving arms of the real Savior, who is greater than all their troubles.

35

Her Name was Parwana

"**M**iss, would you like to buy a beautiful scarf?" a young Afghan girl asked in perfect English, as my colleague and I passed her outside the Italian Embassy.

Her name was Parwana, which means butterfly in Dari.

I immediately noticed she was unlike other children on the street. Most who sold wares were pushy and likely to pickpocket. But Parwana seemed sweet, innocent. I was tempted to buy a scarf from her, but if I did, the other kids, selling anything from plastic flowers to chewing gum, would surround me almost instantly. I smiled at her instead.

"No, thank you," I said.

◈ ◈ ◈

I may have forgotten about Parwana except my colleague recognized her picture in an online news article released a few weeks after we saw her. She had been killed in a bombing near the Italian Embassy.

Bombings in Kabul were becoming more frequent. Two bombs exploded earlier that week, likely killing other beggars. But because of the news article, this one had a name. Parwana stayed on my mind and weighed on my heart as I traveled to a remote mountain region, where my NGO implemented a food-security project for small villages.

During the winter, heavy snowfall cut off the villagers' access to the outside world for at least five months, further diminishing their food sources. Our project had multiple objectives. We employed local men to build erosion-reduction structures on the mountainsides, which allowed water to seep into the ground instead of running into the valleys. This helped increase the farmers' yields, and they could use the cash we paid them for their labor to buy goods for the winter. We also diversified the crops to improve their daily nutrition by giving the women climate-friendly vegetable seeds and teaching them how to plant small gardens.

During my week-long stay, I was invited into the villagers' homes to meet their families. Most of them had never met a foreigner. It was gratifying to put names and faces to the individuals, who I otherwise would have only known by budget codes and employee numbers back in my office in Kabul.

The peacefulness of the village was a salve to my soul. I walked the beautiful high-desert countryside; mountain life was a welcome change from the congested streets of Kabul in which I wasn't allowed to wander. I thought of Parwana, who probably had never stepped outside of Kabul. I imagined her as a butterfly in those hills, spreading her wings in the open air, and enjoying the grandeur of an untouched part of her country where she could finally be free.

36

Long Live Afghanistan

"Today is the beginning of a dream come true," the vice chancellor of the American University of Afghanistan opened her speech.

Two years in the making, that day in early 2014 marked the launch of the business innovation hub, funded by the U.S. government and housed by the American University of Afghanistan in Kabul. The business innovation hub was an accelerator for existing businesses that needed coaching. If the businesses improved, the hub later served as a private investment fund to provide capital to new qualifying businesses.

The business innovation hub believed investing in the for-profit sector was paramount to the long-term future of Afghanistan's economy. International aid to Afghanistan through the non-profit sector had been declining for years. Without international aid the economy suffered.

The owners of the first businesses selected to work with the hub told stories of how they started from nothing and how the hub could take their business to the next level. Private sector development was what brought me to Afghanistan, and seeing Afghans who had taken the risk to start a business was inspirational.

The director of the task force for business and stability operations explained why he enjoyed spending a few weeks a month in Kabul. "When I come to Kabul I get energized. Being in Washington is depressing. No one understands all the good happening in Afghanistan. They just don't get it."

I understood what he was saying. I identified with the feeling of being energized by being in Kabul. And like the vice chancellor, every day I woke up in Afghanistan, I was living out my dream.

Despite the discouraging circumstances all around us, it was a day to look to the future and say, "*Zendabod Afghanistan!*" (Long live Afghanistan)

37

To Be Found in Him

…that I may gain Christ and be found in him …
– Philippians 3: 8-9, NIV

The day was hot and I was grumpy. Smashed in the back seat of a van between a colleague and the door, I regretted getting out of bed. My long coat twisted under me, adding to my discomfort, and my head scarf kept slipping off each time we slammed into potholes. In no mood to talk, I popped in my ear buds and turned up the volume on my iPod.

After dropping off the other passengers I heard a funny sound, even over my music.

"What's that noise?" I asked the driver.

We listened intently and there was an unidentifiable, yet definitely wrong sound coming from our vehicle. The driver pulled over and saw we had a flat tire.

I did not think about my surroundings, too frustrated by the interruption in my busy day. Dripping with sweat, I moved to the empty driver's seat and opened the window.

I left the passenger side door ajar for air flow. Both were a breach of our security policy, and very unwise when stopped on a road well-known for crime.

No one saw him coming. A young man reached into the van and grabbed my purse, then jumped into his getaway ride. I ran after them as they sped off.

Chasing them was my third breach of security. Feeling foolish, I returned to the car without my belongings.

I replayed the episode in my mind for days. I reached for my purse as if it would resurface. I was grasping for the few tangible objects representing my security and comfort: my work ID, phone, wallet, iPod, and some special items I had just brought back from my trip to the U.S – all of them gone in an instant.

Over the next days, I realized what little control I had over my life. If something small could happen suddenly and without my consent, what else could be ahead?

The only security I had was belonging to God. And, really, to be found in Him is all that matters.

38

Struck Down but not Destroyed

abul is home to many foreign restaurants. Their clientele are mainly foreigners and wealthy or well-travelled Afghans. Our favorite was the Lebanese restaurant. The bright, colorful, and clean ambiance made us forget we were in dusty Kabul. And the food was a welcome alternative to our daily fare of rice and beans. Repeat customers often received free appetizers and desserts, which kept us coming back.

In January 2014, attackers entered the restaurant compound through the kitchen, killing first the staff, and then the diners. The owner was on the scene, fighting the attackers until he too was killed.

The event shocked the international community. It was not the first incident at a foreign restaurant, but it was the most brazen. Most organizations reacted by prohibiting their international staff from frequenting foreign restaurants. It was a significant shift in Kabul social life. We adjusted by inviting friends for meals, games, movies, or sporting events televised online and projected onto our living room wall.

One Friday evening in March, we planned to gather in our compound for a poker game. My girlfriends from across town hadn't arrived on time, but I didn't think much of it. When a text message flashed on my cell phone, I figured it was one of them apologizing for being late.

"You probably heard what happened," it said. "Don't worry, we are all safe. No battery left to talk more."

We hadn't heard what happened, so we all checked in with friends to assure they were safe.

While a dozen internationals were having late-afternoon tea at a location where we often gathered for meetings, the compound was attacked. The neighboring compound had armed guards, who fought the assailants, distracting their attention from the original target. My friends escaped with the help of the police, and were escorted to a safe house for the night.

That morning, small groups met across the city in internationals' homes for worship and fellowship. Our group prayed for safety and protection, which was typically not our focus.

As we cancelled the poker game and began putting away the chips, I thought back to our morning prayers. "God, thank you for protecting my friends."

A month later, life felt normal again. My work forced me into a purposeful routine, distracting me from the tragedies. One morning, a security email arrived in my inbox. I occasionally received several in a day, so I didn't give it much attention. Then the subject line caught my eye.

"Attack on International Hospital Ongoing."

My heart pounded, as I read the brief message. Several foreigners, including a doctor, were shot at the hospital entrance.

I knew the hospital. Once, I spent the night there. I took all our new international staff there for routine medical tests.

I knew an American doctor who worked there. I met him and his wife years ago and still saw them on occasion. They were renowned in our Mazar community as people who embodied what it meant to serve Afghans. He only worked at that hospital one or two days a week.

"Maybe today he wasn't there," I thought.

"God, please not Robert," I begged, knowing I had no right to wish it was anyone else in his place.

I couldn't concentrate on my work. I had to find out if the doctor was Robert. As I waited for the news, I had a mounting sense it was Robert.

I was right.

No one in my office knew Robert; it was just another day for them. But for Robert, and the other victims and their family and friends, it was not.

Robert's death impacted me beyond losing an acquaintance. It was difficult to accept that someone who saved many Afghans' lives was the victim of an Afghan. His wife was on television the next day, reiterating how much she and Robert loved Afghans and Afghanistan. She forgave the shooter and asked the world not to judge Afghans by this misguided act. Later, I heard stories from people who were there that day. They had unique opportunities to testify to Christ's love. Something bigger than my short-sighted interpretation happened: God was glorified.

◆◆◆

That summer two foreign women, known by many of my friends, were killed in Herat. When we came together afterwards, we sensed God among us, strengthening our faith and comforting us in our grief. We were struck down, but not destroyed.

◆◆◆

In November, I got a Skype message at work.

"Have you heard what happened in Mazar?"

I knew it would not be good news.

"Cindy died this morning on the way to the hospital."

Cindy was the mother of the American family with whom I shared a compound in my last year in Mazar. Now, her family lived over an hour outside the city, and the closest hospitals were in Mazar.

"What happened?" I asked. Cindy was in her mid-thirties and healthy.

"No one knows the details yet."

After work, I went to my bedroom and cried. I wanted to reach out to Cindy's husband, but it was too soon. A friend in Kabul was part of their organization. She would know what happened and how I could help.

I resolved to call her in a few days. Before I could, a compound in Kabul, belonging to the same organization, was attacked.

I allowed another day or two to pass to give everyone space, then called my friend.

"It's good to hear your voice," she said. "I'm sorry I didn't call sooner, Sonora. I'm just so overwhelmed right now. I was put in charge of cleaning up the yard and house after the attack. It's been awful," she paused, trying to hold herself together.

"Sonora ... I found a finger in the yard."

I closed my eyes. "A finger?"

"Yes, a human finger. Dismembered from the blast."

"My God. I don't know what to say. Is there anything I can do for you?"

We continued talking, and the conversation moved to Cindy and her family. But I didn't ask the details. Cindy was her friend, too, and I didn't want to intrude.

I found it hard to know how to respond to these tragedies. I tried to be thoughtful and patient. I searched for meaningful action and found this: motivation to live every day with love. Each act of kindness, each display of mercy or forgiveness, was building the Kingdom. Evil would not prevail.

39

My Friend the Burqa

I said I would never do it, but I broke my vow. I wore the burqa. It was my last year in Afghanistan, and the security protocol in our new project area in the south required I remain anonymous - so I had no choice. During the car ride from the airport to our base, I envisioned how others would see me. I was accustomed to seeing blue faces peer at me from car windows, and now I was one of them. I felt how I imagined Afghan women feel when they wear the burqa: protected.

For years, I tried to understand the burqa, yet misunderstood it. I wrestled it, detested it, and grieved it. But this time the burqa took me another step into the world I was coming to know more intimately. It assured me we were not enemies.

At lunch with six female Afghan staff, I felt the power of the burqa draw us together. No longer did language divide us - I spoke their language. No longer did culture divide us - I knew their culture. Nothing they said, no story they told, surprised me. I had come to expect their genuine hospitality and care. We were sisters, sitting on the floor, dining off a shared placemat, laughing about who needed to lose weight, and whether eating white foods like yogurt would turn our skin whiter.

I no longer saw the burqa with curiosity, novelty, disdain, or judgment. The years of opening my heart to Afghanistan prepared me to look out from the burqa with a new perspective. It was not a curtain hiding women from the world. It created a place for them to be protected and united. In as much as it served them, who was I to bemoan it? In as much as it didn't serve them, it was their choice to leave behind, not mine.

40

Caregiving

In January 2015, I was back in the project region where we wore burqas, when I got a phone call with instructions to get on the next plane to Dubai. The day before, one of my international teammates had been found unconscious in her bedroom, poisoned by gas from her heater. She spent the night in a hospital in Kabul before she was evacuated to Dubai.

I was sent to Dubai because I was the staff health focal point for the NGO. The practical side of the job was to liaise with the insurance company and make logistical arrangements for the patient and myself. The emotional side required a different kind of energy. I sat with her for days in the dark hospital room, as she battled nausea and headaches. In the moments she felt better, I rubbed her back or talked softly.

I thought about my visits with Anna and the fuzzy pink socks. It wasn't the only time I had been with her in a hospital. Two years after her illness, Anna got appendicitis.

I was part of the rotation of friends who stayed at her bedside after her surgery.

I thought about my housemate in Mazar, who I rushed to the hospital early one morning because she had abdominal pain. The doctor diagnosed her with kidney stones, and she was admitted for more tests and observation. I fell asleep in the bed next to her until the nurse came to insert a catheter. When the nurse turned to me as though I was her next patient, I was too exhausted to speak. My friend had to explain I was a visitor.

As a caregiver I often felt guilty. I was healthy, yet didn't have much strength to offer. I was weary from the accumulating years of unrelenting hardships and heartaches.

41

Nothing New under the Sun

What has been is what will be, and what has been done is what will be done; there is nothing new under the sun.
–Ecclesiastes 1:9, NRSV

Thunk cllllllll pghhhhh thunk. The microphone hit the floor. Static crackled through the loudspeaker, followed by the sound of someone clearing his throat. "Alaaaaaaaaaaaaaaaaaaaaah Akbar" chanted the mullah in his gravelly morning voice.

I heard this sound from my bedroom every morning. The only variation to the year-round pattern was the temperature and amount of daylight. Now in the winter months it was still dark, and cold. In fifteen minutes my alarm would ring; I mentally prepared for my next move.

At the cue of the alarm, I jumped out of bed and changed into my exercise clothes, slippers, and a fleece jacket. I rushed to the bathroom and cringed as I washed my hands in the icy water after using the toilet. I ran back to my room, turned on my computer, loaded my exercise DVD, and put on tennis shoes. I began my workout immediately, so I wouldn't lose motivation and slide back under my warm blankets. My reward was the hot shower when I finished.

Next, I walked down two flights of stairs to my office and put in a full day's work. Although my duties were often the same, the hours passed quickly. After work, I ate dinner, visited with friends, went to sleep and repeated this routine the next day. The days turned to weeks, months, years. The lunar calendar was as familiar to me as the Western one. The pattern of life was governed by the weather: even the terms of war changed with the seasons. The attacks increased when the weather warmed, and didn't subside until the first snow.

The newness of Afghanistan wore off, and with it, the excitement. Feeling caught in the repetition of life, I turned to the Book of Ecclesiastes and read the following words.

"Then I considered all that my hands had done and the toil I had spent in doing it, and again, all was vanity and a chasing after wind, and there was nothing to be gained under the sun" (2:11, NRSV).

I thought about what I had accomplished since coming to Afghanistan. I helped build a business. I learned Dari. I hired and trained administrative staff at the NGO. They were all still works in progress. My toil could continue for years without end. What was ultimately important?

"The last and final word is this: Fear God. Do what he tells you. And that's it. Eventually God will bring everything that we do out into the open and judge it according to its hidden intent, whether it's good or evil" (12:13b–14, The Message).

Success or failure wasn't part of the directive. Just do what God tells you to do.

My journey with God didn't begin or end in Afghanistan. But I had been obedient to His call there. With my deepening dependence on Him, an unshakable relationship was forged that would never be predictable or lackluster.

Printed in the United States
By Bookmasters